By Christopher Dow

Fiction
Effigy
    Book I: Stroud
    Book II: Oakdale
The Books of Bob
    Devil of a Time
    Jumping Jehovah
The Clay Guthrie Mysteries
    The Dead Detective
    Landscape with Beast
    The Texas Troll Unlimited
    Darkness Insatiable
Roadkill
The Werewolf and Tide, and Other Compulsions

Nonfiction
Lord of the Loincloth (nonfiction novel)
Book of Curiosities: Adventures in the Paranormal
Occasional Pilgrimage: Essays on Film, Literature, and Other Matters
Living the Story: The Meandering, True, and Sometimes Strange
    Adventures of an Unknown Writer, Vols. I & II

Poetry
City of Dreams
The Trip Out
Texas White Line Fever
Networks
A Dilapidation of Machinery
Puzzle Pieces: Selected Poems

Art
Harboring with Arabesques: The Art of Christopher Dow

Martial Arts
The Wellspring: An Inquiry into the Nature of Chi
Circling the Square: Observations on the Dynamics of Tai Chi Chuan
Elements of Power: Essays on the Art and Practice of Tai Chi Chuan
Alchemy of Breath: An Introduction to Chi Kung
Leaves on the Wind: A Survey of Martial Arts Literature, Vols. I–VI

Editor
Drifts: Texas Writers: Interviews and Profiles
The Abby Stone: The Poetry of Bartholo Dias
The Best of Phosphene
The Best of Dialog

THE TRIP OUT

THE TRIP OUT

CHRISTOPHER DOW

Phosphene Publishing Company
Temple, Texas

The Trip Out
© 2010 by Christopher Dow
ISBN 13: 978-0-9796968-6-2
ISBN 10: 0979696860

Published by
Phosphene Publishing Company
Houston, Texas, U.S.A.
phosphenepublishing.com

All rights reserved. This book may not be reproduced, in whole or part, without permission from the publisher, except for the use of brief quotations in critical works, articles, or reviews.

The following poems have appeared previously:

"Black Mesa" (*Blonde on Blonde*, February/March 1988)
"Fall Flies" (*Dialog*, Vol. 1, #3, 1983)
"Gray Day" (*Neutron*, 1985)
"Loops" (*Neutron*, 1985)
"Moment" (*T'ai Chi*, Vol. 5, #6, 1981)
"Night Jewel" (*Eternal Echoes*, IV, 1982)
"Out of the Blue" (*Blonde on Blonde*, August 1987)
"Red Ass Spring" (*Neutron*, 1985)
"Rush Hour" (*Appearances*, #7, 1982)
"Science and the Occult" (*Neutron*, 1985)
"The Sedate Leonine" (*Appearances*, #7, 1982)
"The Trip Out" (*Phosphene*, Vol. I, #4, 1979; Reprinted: *Vision Quest*, 1983)
"You Were Wearing Jeans" (*Blonde on Blonde*, August 1987)

Cover Photo: *Brewster County, Texas*, by Tommy LaVergne

For Steve Robinson and Lazaro Aleman
and, of course, Bartholo Dias.

Contents

A Hundred Days in Never-Never Land
Illusive Imagination — 17
You Were Wearing Jeans — 18
Gray Day — 19
Expression — 20
Night Jewel — 21

Trick Guillotine
All Time Compressed — 25
Is He Wise — 26
Incense Stick — 27
Mozart — 28
Shadows in November Sunshine — 29
Disaster Speaks — 30
Moment — 31
Carolers — 32

X-Static
The Wandering Jew — 35
The American Book of the Dead — 36
Sometimes Life — 37
Archaeologists — 38
Stream — 39
Generations — 40
Night Duet — 41
The Door Shut — 42
To Yoko Ono — 43
Some Days — 44
Reprise — 45
We're Always Too Late — 46

CAPTURED BY CANNIBALS
The Sedate Leonine — 49
Gallery Sitting — 50
Reception — 51
Can Poetry Truly Describe the Man? — 52
If Only — 55
For Robert Dante — 56
Out of the Blue — 57
Sunday Afternoon — 59

SHAPESHIFTER
I — 65
II — 66
III — 67
IV — 68
V — 69
VI — 70
VII — 71
VIII — 72
IX — 73
X — 74
XI — 75
XII — 76
XIII — 78
XIV — 79
XV.— 80

RUMMAGING FOR NOTHING
Cruise Control — 83
Float Trip — 84
Roads — 85
Rio Bath — 87

Parched — 88
Big Bend, Thanksgiving — 90
Black Mesa — 91
Red Ass Spring — 92
The Day Is Hot, Still — 93

Psychopomp
Where the Fallen — 99
Religion and the Occult — 100
Science and the Occult — 101
Epitaph — 102
Rush Hour — 103
Reaching Entropy — 104
Loops — 106
Fall Flies — 107

The Trip Out
The Trip Out — 111

THE TRIP OUT

A Hundred Days in Never-Never Land

ILLUSIVE IMAGINATION

Illusive imagination run,
Twisting smoke, wild
Through my mind.
Infuse me with that
Hot-blooded rule, racing
To the sound of tablas in raga
With a tenor saxophone.

I'll never see you again—
But here you are, in the most
Unexpected of places.
Strangeness agitates the scene.
I must be in foreign clothing,
Speaking another tongue.

You Were Wearing Jeans

The sun went down
While you drew it.
I could say you sat
On the brink as you drew. . . .
You were sitting
At the edge of a cliff,
Forty feet to the water's
Stony edge, where swimmers' cries
Drifted up along the shore
With the muted roar of motorboats.
The cliffs across the water softened
After that red ball dropped
Behind the tree-covered hills.
There was a spider in between
Two bushes. She did push-ups
In her web when I touched
Her back with a twig.
The web would rock back and forth,
Back and forth. Why this reaction?
Where lies the defensive mechanism
Behind spider push-ups?
You were wearing jeans,
A yellow shirt with red stripes,
And a green, round hat.
You drew a cactus, too.
Camp fires lit, the last skiers
Took their final bows,
The boats skimmed to berth.
Then it was too late to draw.

GRAY DAY

A gray day on muddy river barrens—
Drift wood, raccoon tracks, muscle shells,
Doomed Indian summer seedlings the only
Litter of life between crumbling wooded
Banks and murky water's sluggish edge.
A distant train sounds rumbling discord
In still air, whistles an aura appropriate
To the melancholy of misty river curves.
But perhaps the river in spring flood
Could not have carried the current's
Soft message that delicate feelings
So often slip away
As unheeded as
Winter water.

EXPRESSION

If I seek a mode of expression
And the heart gets lost in tangles,
Like the right tube of paint
In a cluttered studio?

If I seek a color,
Unplumbed aquamarine pool,
Depths filled to an abstraction
Of light, like yin's eye blazing?

And if I seek the cool water's
Dribbling fingers, trickling energy,
Erosion into channels mimicking
Desire's flow to the heart?

Should I find in my hands
A mystery of crystal or smoke?

NIGHT JEWEL

Just when I thought all
Use for my heart had gone and
Left me in straits
I could not navigate
Even at tide's highest pitch,
An evening occurred I
Never would have anticipated.
Night is the time when
Design's hand overlays the Earth's
Every random frivolity and pain,
Grasps truths we do not.
Across that night design
Revealed the jewel of you.

Trick Guillotine

ALL TIME COMPRESSED

All time compressed
In an instant's disclosure.
Hear and see the world's
Inflection beyond the bounds
Of a second sweep.
There is a world
That goes on long after
The sound is more
Than a thrill of memory,
After the image
Has faded.
I can give you a description:
It is void,
Terror of the plunge,
Ecstasy of flight,
A place of expansion
From the point of a moment.

IS HE WISE

Is he wise who
Is what he means?
Voices rise in anger
From the apartments behind.
When the anger is gone,
There will be laughter.

To them the Voice
Is a breath of wind
Over a distant mountain
Called Time.

When Time is mentioned,
The telephone rings
A dozen times.

Incense Stick

A stub of incense stick
Found jammed in the latch
Of a trunk packed for years
Around town.
Lit, it shuttles me back
To the time of flowers,
Of bouquets of youth
Dressed in mind and heart
Colors, of new horizons—
The time of vibrant days
And heavy, hectic nights.
And then the stub begins
To burn out.
Though the scent retains
The fragrance of dreams,
There now begins to intermix
The pungent odor of wood
Burning from the status
Of support to ash.
Then the small stick
With one blackened tip
Goes into the ashtray.

MOZART

Mozart, small dog, wild hair.
Nothing could contain him.
He could escape
From any back yard.
Once got a call
From a woman
In the next neighborhood.
He was in her back yard,
Making music with her poodle.
She couldn't understand
How he got in.
Showed me the four-foot
Chain-link fence. I laughed.
I'd seen him climb
Eight-foot ones for sport.
Should have named him Houdini—
It only took him a year
To escape from life.

SHADOWS IN NOVEMBER SUNSHINE

Early November sunshine on the driveway
Viewed from the second story window—
The roof's shadow a slanting contradiction
That sprouts a lattice memory of trees.
Movement—two shadow squirrels chase
One another in noiseless encounter
From one cipher branch to another.
On the pavement beneath,
A gray tabby strolls from light to shade,
Oblivious to the antics above him.
In the other room she was playing
With the squirrels, tapping on the glass.

DISASTER SPEAKS

Disaster speaks in liquid tongues,
Pours into cavities and recesses
Where cold reason's slave
Immobilizes it in frozen clarity.
As dear things are,
It is a mirror if not
Shattered.
Can you see
Yourself in all the pieces?

MOMENT

In the spread of the bird's tail
There is a moment like the warrior's
Dance of ten thousand tears.
The march must continue.
The winds of change....

CAROLERS

A mysterious knock.
No one calls this late
Unannounced, so quietly,
So without warning.
They sang softly, simply,
Word sheets lit
With subdued flashlights.
I don't remember what they sang.
Something light for the first,
Something striking deeper
Chords for the second.
I don't remember their faces.
It seems like they were a little
Embarrassed that I cried.

X-Static

THE WANDERING JEW

The Wandering Jew is just
Reality's janitor,
Waiting
For the party to finish
So he can clean up
And go home, too.

THE AMERICAN BOOK OF THE DEAD

The American Book of the Dead
Is a gun catalog.

SOMETIMES LIFE

Sometimes life
Is like those giveaway
Pens that ask you
To compare the numbers
Printed on the pen
With numbers on a telegram.
If the numbers match, you win.
Big cash. Trouble is
No one ever sends
A telegram, and the pens
Don't work or write purple.

ARCHAEOLOGISTS

Archaeologists
Compulsively keeping house
In ancient buildings.

STREAM

Beneath crumbling banks
Rushing waters erode earth,
Wash new lands downstream.

Trees precipitate
Over the edge, hang in slow
Slides to swift currents.

GENERATIONS

Earlier generations saw
The future as vast,
With many wide, planed surfaces
In dustless, machined perfection.
Instead, it's just cluttered.

NIGHT DUET

Night duet—cats
Howling territorial
Prerogatives.

THE DOOR SHUT

The door shut
As he walked into
The night.
A million things
Could have happened
To him on the way home,
But none of them did.

TO YOKO ONO

I looked, saw your eye
In the darkest shadow of
An iris blossom.

Some Days

Some days is cruisin',
Some days is bruisin',
Some days ya wanna stay home.

But when the heat's up,
Ya can't put yer feets up,
Ya jus' got to breathe deep and go on.

REPRISE

Drift doomed.
Crumbling, murky
Discord shrouds
Appropriate abandon.
Curves flood:
Slow,
Delicate,
Away.

We're Always Too Late

We're always too late
When we're on time—
Just a whistle-breath past
On an outbound.

Captured by Cannibals

THE SEDATE LEONINE

The sedate leonine drowses
On the brink of darkness
And revelation,
Couched in his domain,
Coupling introspective consideration
To the gregariousness of the world.

We are such small motes
Constructing such gigantic dreams.
The universe would be filled
By as few as one,
And one dream by all the motes.
We construct our castles in air
And their spires become
The vehicles of our lunacy.
The moon is our sister, and we,
As affected by her as she by us,
Ride the willful tides
Of her crazy creations.
We use her as the base
For further explorations
Into the space of our lives.

GALLERY SITTING

Gallery sitting over Old Market Square.
A truck pulls up to deliver
Linen to the restaurant downstairs.
Business clothes eat in the restaurant.
In the park across the street, bums
Sit on artificial hillocks created
By the Parks Department, watching
Doug and Billy, two artists, toss
A Frisbee and play with Doug's dogs.
Across the square, against overcast
And a brisk breeze heralding winter,
Rises a new multistory parking garage,
Obliterating one more historic building,
One more piece of sky. The towering crane
Constantly swings across the horizon.
Beneath it, farther reaching, atop
The low roof of the locals-only hangout,
A satellite dish sweeps the heavens
For different signals. The artists leave.
The linen truck leaves. Business clothes
Vanish into rags as bums come over to rifle
Garbage cans left out by the restaurant.
Darkness falls over the square.

RECEPTION

There is a wedding
Reception in a pavilion—
Cement floor, tin roof,
Supports of steel.
Adults group at one end,
Eating, talking.
At the other end
Two children play.
A girl dressed
In a one-piece
Swimsuit kicks
At a puddle,
Skimming the surface
With the sole of her foot,
Spraying the smooth
Water into the air.
The boy chases a tennis
Ball he has thrown
Lightly across the cement
Floor to catch
This object of his own
Impulse at the other side.

CAN POETRY TRULY DESCRIBE THE MAN?

Too far to see any features
But his spectacles.
He walks, stops on the sunlit
Bank next to the pond.
He has a chrome-glinting
Stick in his left hand.
It is a cane, a golf club.
I cannot tell.
He stands there, leaning
On it, looking around.
Few people here in the park
Late on a weekday.
No one is near, no one
Watching, I imagine he thinks,
Not noticing me across the pond,
On a stone bench shadowed beneath trees.
He unfolds the top of the stick
And sits down. He is sitting
On the chrome stick.
It is one of those walking-stick
Seats that fold out.
So Prussian.
Something is not right.
He rises, leans forward, looks
Between his legs at the seat.
Arms behind his back, he shakes it,
Sits back down, shoves it
With both hands.

His seat is still not right.
He stands up, gripping the seat
With both hands behind him,
Raises it up, jams it down.
Losing his balance, tottering
Precariously on one leg,
He sits down roughly,
Shoving and pushing.
He stops moving.
Is it right?
He is too far forward.
He hunches himself up and back,
Now more leaning backwards
Than sitting, using the seat
As a crutch for his ass.
A flying buttress.
He looks around. No one
He sees has seen his struggles.
He still does not see me.
He looks down,
Notices his front shirttail
Has come out in his struggles,
Stuffs it back in.
Looks around.
He looks bored.
He has a seat of portable comfort
From which to watch,
But out on the bank
All he can see are
A few scraggly ducks
Paddling lukewarm muddy water.
The perspective is wrong.

Besides, he hasn't the patience
For scenes of nature.
He sits for some minutes,
Twisting his hands and fidgeting,
Then rises and stands and folds
The seat, and again it is a walking stick
Dangling from his left hand.
It doesn't work well for that, either—
The handle is too thick and the seat
Too bulky. But he is determined.
He walks around a bit,
Jauntily swinging the cane,
Before walking becomes
As uncomfortable as sitting.
He has come all this way
To discover the failures of his device.
He leaves.

IF ONLY

If only we could have known
When we looked at all the shining
Faces grouped in youthful harmony
How hard it was in the world,
How the little things would add up
To impossible conclusions, to dreams
Dimmed by habits, blindness, and fatigue.
If only we could have seen
How the faces would change.

For Robert Dante

Cigarette smoke curls,
Liquid pain
In rarefied air,
And you sit
Like some djinn
On a distant cloud,
Worrying with traffic
Bugs on asphalt tape
That oil spread
Until your nerves fray....
As if travel
Is too slow a conveyance.

OUT OF THE BLUE
(for Ralph)

Famous film personality
Detonates on the northside.
Nihilistic flickering images
Give way to hot seat—
Silver foil-covered frame
Concealing six sticks.
Dynamite. Famous film
Personality walks onto the wet
Clay of the speedway track
Where only minutes earlier
Hurtling steel and engine thunder
Split the night's chill
With the thrill of spinout and victory.
Apotheosis and indulgence hang
On the amplified announcements,
Limp in the oily air.
"The Russian Dynamite Death Chair Act.
Famous Hollywood personality.
Would the flagman come out
And flag him as he comes down?"
A wrecked school bus began
The movie, and it ended in dynamite.
The crowd comes in school busses.
The personality crouches in the chair,
Police move the expectant crowd back,
Behind the telephone poles.
He lights a match.

The wind blows it out.
He lights another.
The wind blows it out.
He lights the whole pack,
And there is a flare of sparks.
The breezy air goes silent....
Then we are all slapped
By an invisible hand, yelled at
Thunderously, and the personality
Spasms like Wile E. Coyote
In a cloud of light and dust,
At one with pressure, heat, and sound
Too powerful to endure for more than a moment.
Then the crowd rushes forward,
Into the cloud of settling dust,
And the famous Hollywood personality
Emerges from the swirling murk
And stands unharmed, eyes glazed
With the thrill of spinout and victory.

Sunday Afternoon

What is frustration?
It's hitting walls with the cracked
Knuckles and pulpy flesh of hands
That have need to create but all
Too often only seem to damage themselves.
It sits in baser motives, begets
Cruelty to pets, coldness to family,
The need to abandon all associations
Of a past full of frustrations.
The worst part is the emptiness
When the anger is gone.
Frustration is a koan that brings
Enlightenment's naked brother, obscurity.

Needing to relieve the weight,
Perspective, and tension
That makes all the world heavy
And impossible to abide,
I drove through the beautiful day,
Hoping the sunshine might dispel
The darkness lowering on the horizon.
But the city ambiance, so familiar,
Became a pressing alien fist,
Squeezing my breath out, squeezing
Me with too many memories. Everywhere
I looked there were sights tainted
With failures of the past.
The very clearness of the sky, heat
Of the sun mocked my disappointments.

So I drove out, had to leave the crush,
Needed the feeling of motion, needed
The feeling of belonging to the wind.
Past monuments of steel and glass bones,
Past concrete overpasses that pass
Over but go nowhere, past
Cemetery suburbs, past dead dogs—
Or were they only sleeping
In ditches by the roadway?
Miles away, when thought returned
From that clouded place where all
Shapes are vague and threatening,
I found a bridge and sat.

Let me describe it because
What we find is so linked to what we are.
It is an old bridge, a little way off the road,
Twenty feet long, its timbers smelling of pitch—
A farmer's bridge between fields,
Never intended for traffic heavier
Than implements of cultivation,
Now too weak to be crossed except on foot.
It spans a drainage ditch, weeded slopes dropping
Eight feet to murky, unmoving, muck-bottomed water.
At one end stands a beehive, buzzing life, sweet nectar
Gleaned by drops from abundant wildflowers
Of yellow, white, and purple.
Beyond the hive spreads
A field of young corn and blue space.
On the other side, weeds fallow a field.
It is a bridge that goes nowhere across
A stagnant slough wafting with decay.

Silver minnows flash in the clouded
Water, dodging and playing
With crawdads and skimming water beetles.
What sustenance do they find in this muddy pool?

When I sat down, I lost my pen cap,
Dropped it into the water
Where it became like
A satellite fallen on another world—
Alien to these aquatic creatures
That have no thought beyond
This muggy pool of silver flashes
And flip of crawdad tail.
I have fled the alien city
To drop alien, plastic debris into nature—
That is the nature of frustration.

This is really a sort of peaceful
Spot, between fields.
The distant traffic is only a hum,
Barely more than the nearby hive.
I sit on this bridge, with the sun
Warming my back and breeze cooling my face,
And after a long time
Feel my tensions drain into the clear air
To be carried off on the wings of the insects
That leap and flit and buzz in the weeds.

Frustration is sitting on this welcome bridge
In this beautiful day out in nature,
And after letting nature soothe
Away my ragged edge, realizing

That the two ugly-looking
Lumps in the water thirty feet from the bridge
Are decrepit dog carcasses surrounded
By flashing fins and snapping pinchers
That tear them to frenzied shreds.
It's realizing that death is the only
Source of life in our clouded pool.
When I throw a few pebbles
At the crawdads' carrion consensus,
Something large and unseen splashes
In the deepest part of the pool,
Chilling me despite the sun's warmth.
Perhaps my pen cap will adorn its shrine.
I wade through the weeds, back to the car.
All too soon I see the city skyline.

Shapeshifter

I

I talk to the world's hair,
And I talk softly because
I am on foreign ground,
Where human sight
Occurs spontaneously.
If you exercise it,
Will it increase?
As do muscles,
As do emotions,
As does will.
And yet we furnish the apartments
Of our complexes
With standardized forms,
Inhabit them with conventional formulas.
Individuality is the privilege
Of getting leaked.
Are not we all fodder?
Or the blessing?
Fantasies, fantasies.
Realities should be so
Much stranger, so much more terrible,
So much deeper and more filled.
I talk softly because
I am on foreign ground.

II

How much do you know?
How much incense have you felt
At the ire of the Earth's passions?
How can you feel
Ignorant in the face of the great
Up and down, the push and pull
And push, the never-ending battle,
The famous dichotomies?
The terror of the night?
Time?

III

The catatonic sat
In his chair.
It's all pointless, he thought,
Waiting to be sucked back
Into the general delusion
Where the results of actions
Intentionally done are not
As interesting as the effects
On a world written
In first person omnipotent.

My abuse is for myself.
I abuse only myself.
I am my own abuse.
Abuse is my only self.
Self is my only abuse.
For abuse, myself.
But I will not fall into
The fallacy of nothing,
For nothing is fallacy,
And nothing is too simple
For the simple nothing.

Not perfect, it is
The place of perfection:
The omnipresence of one object,
The omnipotence of one action.

IV

Physical description:
Mannerism, twitch,
Betrayal of emotion,
Glint in the eye.
Yes, remain in light.
Burn. Illuminate your
Section of the path.
Go on leaving your
Body in air.

V

When is a mile not a mile?
When is Buddha on the road?
When are the days to be
Filled, the nights full?
But your ear knob is playing,
"Put me down, put me down."

VI

Is all talk an altered crying,
Imitation of first speech
From the mouth that speaks worlds?
The creative urge—
Resplendent pain,
Loss's gain,
Spirit on the verge where
Hurry breeds hurry
For motion's own sake.
We act as if there's
A race to be won.
We *are* the race,

And the sorrow of things
That cannot be erased.

VII

The floor rocks,
The walls
Tilt at the prospect
Of shifting reality.
Poetry just sublimates
The process, alters it,
Dams it,
Slows it
To speed
Of pen.

VIII

A bastard and a whore
Sat by the sea.
"Bitch," said the one,
"Have some tea."
She sat for a moment,
Then shook her head.
"Thank you," she said,
"No more for me."

Knowledge isn't a painful process—
Rather it's the opposite.
Perhaps when I'm old
And have nothing to lose
I'll dispense with the clues,
Get out in the cold
With the one who knows it
Isn't contained in a closet.

IX

One of my more esoteric friends claimed that people alive in the United States today are actually reincarnations of the people of the Roman Empire. His arguments had a ring of truth, circumstantial though they were. One argument cited similarities in the preponderance of large coliseum-type events. Yes, I thought, coliseums, Astrodomes, Superdomes. Only now they throw lions to the Christians.

x

Windblown
Across a watery waste,
He passed islands
Of crystalline distress,
Plucked jeweled bouquets,
And flung them into constellations
That mariners might gain bearings
On seas without charts,
Without beacons.

XI

Oh, the Light!

Oh, the Light!

Oh, the Light!

Oh, the Light!

Oh, the Light!

XII

In the golden light
We went to a show
About a man with only
One arm and no legs
Luckily the remaining arm
Was the dominant one,
Was complete,
And his head
Had not received
A single scratch.
The man had a nice pension,
A secretary, and numerous
Other restitutions.

After the show,
At an intersection
Where the streets
Lay in darkness,
We saw one man
Hold up another man,
And money in one hand,
Gun in the other,
He walked away.
But the other
Drew a knife and threw it
Into the robber's back, at which
The robber turned and fired
And missed and the thrower threw

Again and the knife struck through
The robber's cheek and into his
Head, and he began to moan, and his
Eyes sought in the darkness
For the knife thrower, and he shot
At shadows and moaned that moan,
Then ran out of bullets
And staggered off into darkness.
We heard that moan days later,
Masquerading as the wind.

XIII

A cat scratches its ear—
The stately majesty of nature,
The gritty reality.

Life is not much different than a mirror
That feels the tragedy of its own reflection—
For which all things are real and possible,
Yet which is easily shattered
And always has things backwards.

XIV

The nadir of terror swaying
Over the abyss of certainty, above
Hell's gate, shook my stride—
The Earth's tremor contained within
One point/instant.
And it's all paranoid glass panes,
Peering recesses, breath on curtains.
Breathing in my ear.
Soft.
I love your image.
And the washer is booked up,
And shoulders hunch beneath
The cold dusk's eyes,
Bundling a bag of laundry dirty
With the residue of manners.
You look so kind.
You are kind?
Please be kind to me....

XV

And what had it come to
This life of dreams
Where dreams of life
Are no less real?
I want to rest not in sleep
Of pleasant dreams,
Nor in dreamless sleep,
But only in awakened days
When tremors pass resistless
Through the terror of abandon.
Who orders the spheres?
When is the day to become
Night's precursor, night's
Blessing, night's brother?
And they said it was good.
It was good. It was good.
And they told of success.
Great success. Good success.
But they failed to warn
The children that they were,
Themselves, children.
And they made of the children
Their own images.

Rummaging for Nothing

CRUISE CONTROL

Driving a cruise control
Truck, trailing the smut
Of cities across
The ever-changing terrain
Of central Texas,
Driving the route
Of the pioneer,
The Army of the Republic.
From the swelter of insect
Thicket lying in
The Gulf's hollow, across
To the chapel
Of Santa Anna's Indian Summer,
Up in climbing undulation north
To the edge of rocky rawness,
Then back down in a sloping
Slide that tapers to a long
Crawl just before it empties
Into the Gulf.
We follow the seasons
And watch the skies for rain.

FLOAT TRIP

Once upon a river
Were hundreds of inner
Tubes, colors, and gaiety
The cold water could not quench.
An aural banner of cries
From those splashed
With drops singing
Of deep, dark aquifers
Drifting mercurial current
Hovered above the urban flotsam
Jettisoned with polarized eyes,
Ice chest life supports, bobbing
Bottles of sunscreen.
It was like a leisurely freeway.
We even rode on tires.
Where else to pass the holiday
But at home away?
Where else to be at leisure
Where at home one must be unrelenting?
Whoever heard of friendly banter
Between stalled lanes of rush hour?
There it's not a good idea
To roll down the window.
Here, with shielding steel removed,
We are all equally at the current's
Mercies. We all burn
In the unvarnished sunlight.

ROADS

I want to talk about the road,
To write down paved ribbons,
Passing cars like words edited from thought.
I want to talk about change
And the highway that goes and goes,
That doesn't stop at the sea,
Across which deer leap,
Upon which rocks fall, curved, straight,
Slicing through this life, this countryside
Of billboard promises
Of new sights, a future, delights.

It's strange to steer along adamant imperatives
Thinly laid across an unobstructed universe.
It's odd to consider a paved path home—
A home that never stops, is never still,
A home that always leads away then back to home.
I like the way highways cross rivers,
The way currents only pass
But never meet and merge to ponder similarities.

I drive the highway to you, away. Who are you?
I could drive forever and never know
More than the only constant, change.
Here's Brenner's, used to be Nickerson Farms.
Here's a small car used to be a large one.
Here's a burned patch used to be green.
Here's a road one day will be forgotten.

Here's a river one day will run dry.
Here is a man no longer young.

When I travel the road for long
Distances at high speeds, I feel
My spirit attenuate out behind me
For miles, like a jet contrail—
A streak of my being that only
Catches up hours after I've stopped.

Once I reflected on eternity,
Now I merely journey by steps,
Looking at the few road signs,
Following meager maps.
All the flows reflect change—
The road, the river, sex, eating,
The growth of trees.
But are all these flows really change
Or merely semblances, shadows
To trick the unwary,
Bartering physical motion
For the wealth of eternity?

But in all things that reflect
The eternal, there is truth
That can set one free.
The invisible ambience of death
Hovers in patches above the road
Like a mirage's promise.
The road is dry, then wet, curving
Then straight, sloping up and down.
And when the change is over,
It's still the same road.

RIO BATH

Dive in, flat, shallow,
Slightly sideways from
The rock wall, deep breath,
River's brown turbulence closing
Over head in a cooling tussle.

Slide downstream.
Swim with the current
Strong at the feet,
Flow pushing against,
Gliding over and under,
Undulating, twisting and arrowing,
Liquid pressure tensing at arm's
Slightest winging of watery flight.

A few strokes, then,
To lie in the gentle brown
Bosom of an eddy, careful
Only to keep head above water.
Drift up, carried back, then

Up and over the rock wall into
The 110-degree swelter of the
Hot spring, sliding feet
First into the heat.
Ahhh....

PARCHED

I was walking
Along a river
Of a southern desert
Where it empties
Into a basin
From a beachless gorge
Of vertical rock and
Fast moving water.
Lying there were many
Colored rocks, and I
Searched among these
Natural miniatures
For my heart's desire.
Van Gogh, Picasso,
Magritte, even Leonardo,
All in Nature's inimitable
Progression of shades and tones.
She laughed at me
With a rose, a finger,
A smiling face,
And a man entranced
By a vision holding him immobile.
I took the rocks
From the water, and they dried
Rapidly in the hot breeze,
Lost the wraiths of color
And form revealed when wet.
These were but beginnings,

A thousand times more eloquent
Than my vision could ever possess.
And I looked up
To the cliff's towering rim
And saw castles of guileless art
As real and sharp
As the blasting sun,
As smooth as the river's
Inexorable flow cutting
Through the cleft.
Those cliffs rest on foreign land,
So seeking shelter, then,
From the sun and desert heat
I climbed miles
Into the mountains behind.
But in those mountains
No water lies,
And one must carry
At sweat's purchase
All one's supply.
And as I climbed,
I thought of the river
And its coolness under
The blazing desert sun,
And the ruined adobe
Structures dotting its banks.
I thought, ah, for a taste
Of that wet coolness now....
But I was parched.

Big Bend, Thanksgiving

Most adaptable—
Man.
In stark places perched
Leeward,
Protected beneath layers
Nature
Provided only under
Duress.
Amidst desolate brown,
Showers,
Lowering skies, and cold
Winds
Are the bright colors
Brought.

BLACK MESA

Ancient gray ash clay
Dried to brittle cement,
Strewn with iron rocks
Burned black by
Volcanic winds.
Whole basins
Where the rusty stuff
Intermixes with
Rocks of every color
And rocks within rocks
Within rocks—
Egg within egg within.
In this wild desolation,
Something left turds
Outside our tent
In the night.

RED ASS SPRING

Verdant wash
Of many trickles,
Circle of stones,
Old rusty can,
Miniature cliff dwellings.
All that could be seen
From the desert floor
Was the giant cottonwood.
Up close, it's huge,
Bark three inches thick,
Trunk five feet through.
Just below, water
Pooled in red clay
Before disappearing
Into the sandy soil.
While we were here
The tree blinked
And missed us.
Here we are more
Transient than the wind.

The Day is Hot, Still

The day is hot, still.
I sit on a jut
Of hardened mud,
A tiny peninsula
In a lake's small cove.
Shade covers me now,
Though soon the sun
Will bake my seat.
Out, past the sunline,
The lake's surface shimmers,
But closer,
On the shaded water,
Midges swarm, darting sharp
Legs across a smoother surface.
A foot down at the edge
A shape is threateningly
Half-concealed—a face,
A dangerous beast,
A shadow unknown.
My dreams are disturbing.
Only work keeps my thoughts
As calm as the surface
Of this little cove.
With no work,
Midges run wild
Above half-imagined shapes
Beckoning from the depths.
I do not wish

To use occultism
As an excuse for
Erratic behavior,
Vagaries of emotion
And temperament.
What is disturbing
Me here in this simmering
Calm, with only
The buzz and chirp
Of insect life
And occasional plop
As something goes into
The water?

A beautiful electric
Blue dragonfly comes
To let me look.
Intricate tracery,
Living mechanism,
Tiny head. No room
For brains.
Yet it lives, copulates,
Dies. No problem.
It is a tiny dragonfly,
And there are tiny midges
Scurrying on the water,
Tiny spiders, tiny fish,
And bugs so tiny
They're almost invisible.
Near my feet
A tiny plant pokes
Through the naked mud.
It must take a lifetime

To calm from
The trauma of birth.
When I bend,
I see lots of tiny
Plants poking through
The naked, baked mud.
The dragonfly likes me
But won't land
On my finger,
Let me examine it.
I'm probably
Sitting on lots
Of tiny things.

A breeze ruffles the water,
Scuds clouds across the sky,
Cools the air.
The sun now touches
The end of the tiny peninsula
With fingers of light,
Soon will bathe it hotly.
It's time to move
For I can't get
Attached to this place.
Its calm is too small, too
Hard, too baked, too surrounded
By simmering shimmer,
And I will only crush
Its tiny life.
As I go, I leave shoe
Prints by day old
Deer tracks.

Psychopomp

WHERE THE FALLEN

Where the fallen
Flowers go, there
Goes each
Footfall, every
Breath's atmospheric
Change. If time
Heals forgotten wounds—
Complex dreams open
To the scourge of tears—
Do simpler purposes
Lance the blemish
With which the heart
In eruption ulcerates
It's vivid paper skin?
Where the fallen
Flowers go I know
Not but that we
Walk in atmospheric
Time, breathe, and change.

RELIGION AND THE OCCULT

And the Lord said,
"Let there be light!"
And there was light
And it was good.
Then the Lord walked
Around the room, got
What he came for,
And left.
As he shut the door
He said,
"Let there be darkness!"
And there was darkness
And it was good.

SCIENCE AND THE OCCULT

A caveman
Enters the room.
The electric light
On the ceiling is off.
He climbs a chair,
Demolishes the light
Trying to make it work.
The caveman steps down,
Sees the switch
On the wall,
Tries it without success.
He leaves the room convinced
Electricity does not exist.

Epitaph

The store clerk was murdered by robbers.
The store owner said they were black guys,
As if the clerk died because
They were black, not killers.

In the air over the ferry,
A flock of gulls swayed and dipped
For the food tossed from the deck
By children delighted at the antics.
On one bird a bright orange spot draws
The eye to attention. The bright
Day dims, the children's happy cries
Become like cries of hate.
The orange spot is a plastic bead
On the end of a blowgun dart
That completely pierces through
The body of the hapless bird.
The gull sways and dips with the others,
Desperate with the others
To snatch the food,
To catch one more day of life
From the air before it falls into the sea.
But with its wing cramped
In pain against its body
It cannot maneuver to get its share.

Pay your price, get your change.
Man is like a stray animal.
Life, oh God, shadows of a dream.

Rush Hour

As night's darkness flows
Into cities, a force flows
In too. The only escape is to
Lock yourself in a metal capsule,
And ride the current, pushed out by
The entering pressure of the force.
Everyone watches their rearview mirrors
Apprehensively, to see if they are being
Followed.

REACHING ENTROPY

Time enters the stream of conscious
Effort toward anti-entropic impulses
And highlights their futility
With pervasive decay.
Still, we strive and build castles,
Write words, and feed our bodies
To history's tuneless hiss that says
Once, for a while, then never again.

Seduced by endless possibilities—
Youth's ageless and fickle mistress—
We blindly love towering cities, new
Music, and rockets to the moon
As symbols of our personal growth,
Only later to find our mistress
In another bed.
She loves youth,
Not the body of its work.
Ever faithful to growth,
Faithless to old frontiers,
She approaches, pauses, passes on,
Leaving a fertility symbol behind
To reside in our memory,
Carrying our single seed in her womb.

By that means we can bar the door
To the pressures of time and the knowledge
Of a death that is imminent,

Inevitable, and entropically total.
For though our bodies die,
Our ideas become supplanted,
And the paper of our writings disintegrates,
And though the future holds endless
Ruin, streams of dust, shifting continents,
New oceans, and darkness punctuated by
Sol's exploding supernova,
We feel the thrill of growth within us,
Of endless flights of steps reaching.
We witness that life defies
Entropy, if only for a short while—
That knowledge and spirit become ever
Greater in the face of entropy's challenge.
Strangely enough, the evidence dwells in time.

LOOPS

I
We travel the road.
It is the time of captives.
What is the time between the light
And the last source?
Where are the mountains?
Too often we turn in,
Too often we put our epitaphs
On the stone slabs we presume
Are something final.
Our perceptions are limitations
Defining the chaos about us.
It goes from the word...
It goes from limitation,
From reason's need to pass beyond
Existence in which freedom is ultimate
And for which we pine
In moments of dismay.

II
Time's points of reference are calibrated
To the nanosecond correspondent
To the cycles. Are they twenty-four?
Who has done this?
We all play with toys.
Time. What is time but a point
Beyond which we cannot identify
The urges we feel?

Fall Flies

Black speck on the wall—
Closer—Fly. Fat fly.
Buzz from the left, at the window
To sunlight and green early fall.
Three fat early fall flies.
With no malice, I
Shake a finger in the air
One inch over the wall-bound one.
Don't fly, I say in my mind. Just
Let me shake my finger at you.
It does not fly. I shake.
I turn to those others,
Silhouetted against nature,
All fat and easy to squash.
One crouches, the next buzzes
A bit in the air, the third
Walks up the left window molding,
Buzzing, under a shimmering thread.
Another thread. Another. Spiderweb.
My eyes range up past the crawling fly,
To the upper corner of the window.
Over the body of a fly, a spider
Hunches. The fly is fresh and fat.
The spider touches and sucks.
Fat fly. The others buzz
In sporadic bursts against the window.
The one on the wall lobs itself
Through the air to the glass,
Thumping a landing on that surface.
The world a movie at its feet, it waits

In early fall's dappled warmth,
A fat fly with other fat flies,
Waiting for the freedom of night,
When bright panes do not
Mesmerize with illusions of escape,
When cool drafts lend
A ride to winged creatures
Through a world of darkness
And no transparent barriers.

The Trip Out

The Trip Out

Rolling down to the desert
In the cruise control
Truck, past the violet litter
Of bluebonnets and Indian paintbrushes
Strewn along the roadsides.
As speed maintains,
The royal color yields
To the coarseness of scrub,
And the convolutions of sediment
Laid lightly over the past
Are exposed to my sight.
As the thin skin of sand
Succumbs to the bouldered jumble
Of nature's stonemason's frivolity,
I feel the influences covering my life
Begin to strip from me as they tangle
In the wind and branches
Of the scrub, baring
The bones of my truer feelings.

The strip of metal
Crossing the Pecos is the bridge
Between life and death.
To the west the desert truly
Begins. Water is power,
And life is as dry as death.
We stand on the catwalk,
Twenty-five feet beneath the roadbed,

In the center of the superstructure,
With the wide and rugged-banked
Flow's power far beneath us.
The wind rushes by our ears,
Pushes and tugs at our bodies.
The mass of water, so far below,
Surges and thrums its power
Up the concrete pilings, through
The superstructure, and into
The structures of our skeletons.
All around is a nervous clamor of steel
As vehicles pass overhead.
From our vantage we clearly see
The black mouth of an Indian's cave
From which archaeologists removed
Bones and artifacts—the possessions
Of an earlier traveler.

What I have left behind
I can never return to,
For when I return, the perceptions
That trail in Hansel and Gretel
Crumbs behind this vehicle will
Have been torn by the brush
And carried off by the wind.
I will not be able to grasp
Them in more than memory's
Greasy grip, and they will be gone,
The shreds drying in hot serenity
On the slaking volcanic sands.
These sands will return with me,

Will hang for months in pockets,
Will become part of the dust of my life.

Then we are where cruise
Controls do not exist,
Where wind-blown dust
Seeps into everything and grits the skin.
We camp at Solis, and there seek comfort
Along the banks of the rio
Whose meandering brown water lends
Cool humidity to the air beneath
The shelter of cane and mesquite forests.
It is a place lacking mystique,
Of few restless spirits, a place
To cry of the emptiness
Of tracts so populated by the past
Their psychic spaces are replete,
And nothing can be injected.
It is a place where those cries
Are sucked out, sucked up,
And are gone.

Later, after miles of rough dirt road
That stumbles over barren hills
And twists through gravelly arroyos,
We come upon a structure
That protrudes from a hillside
Like the bones of an ancient creature
Or a metamorphosis of the earth.
It is an abandoned mercury mine.
Here cinnabar was dug

From dangerous veins,
Brought to the surface,
And cooked in a huge, elaborate mazework
Of stone, cement, and brick furnaces
To extract its quicksilver blood.
How strange that mercury's elusive
Substance and mutable nature
Can be distilled only by such concrete means.

Next camp is at Talley.
We hike for a day across
Parched and ragged land
Carrying our burdens on our backs,
Counting the items of our baggage,
Calculating their bulk, weight, necessity.
We stop in some rare shade,
Sip water, rest, and rising,
Discover some of our burden gone.

The days pass.
I look at my skin.
Every time I'm here,
I burn.
Each time, I become
More naked than before.

Then we move deeper
Into the desert.
It is hot, dry, and dusty.
Even back near the river,
The wind stirs the dust
And blows it over everything.
That which survives here

Survives by staying on top
Of the sand's shifting patterns,
Lives on by moving always.
If the wind would sometimes cease,
Perhaps the sand would not
Cover the unmoving or blow into my eyes.
If the sun did not burn down,
It may be that I would not become
As brown as an Indian who left
His bones and artifacts in some cave.
If the rock, cactus, and scrub
Did not conspire to strip pretense
From me, then likely I would
Use them for those ragged
And brambly qualities.

We set out from Abajo,
Once a creek-side community,
Once alive, now just crumbled adobe.
Rude, sometimes fallen wooden crosses
Mark twenty rock-covered graves.
Across the creek begin clay and rock flats
Scarred with gullies, punctuated
By wind-worn hills and ridges, dotted
With cactus, mesquite, sage, and odd pockets
Scooped out of hillsides and littered
With chunks of adobe.
Who, seventy years past,
Dug these hovels, farmed, and died?
Perhaps a single man.
Can you see him work,
Digging in the hot sun,
Miles from any town,

Years from the salvation of shade,
Lost to the fabric of abundant water
So threadbare and holy here?

After hours of trudging the flats, scrambling
In and out of arroyos, and weaving our way
Among the hills and ridges, ahead
Appears the locale of our search—a canyon.
This canyon would be an enigma anywhere,
For even in the strongest, brightest sunlight
It is a dark scar torn up the side of the mesa.
Even in the shining heat it has an alien coolness.
Beginning as a perpetual trickle of runoff
Water from the mesa table, it falls
Down the mesa wall in a thousand-foot
Gash until it hits the talus slope.
There it widens, and huge, water-gouged overhangs
Stretch out on either side of the cliff wall.
There, also, begins the jumble of rocks and immense
Boulders that spreads in an ever-widening
Cascade for half a mile down the face of the mesa
To the desert floor, where the torrential rains
So famously dangerous in dry regions
Have eaten a deep, wide crescent
From the softer earth, after depositing
And redepositing the boulders above.
In dry times, only a trickle of water runs
Down the gash to disappear in the sand
Of the talus slope, and remarkably,
Here, miles from any water but this trickle,
Thousands of wasps daub the mud of the slope
To create an insectual parody of ancient
Indian cliff dwellings along the inner

Curvatures of the water-gouged cliffs.
The boulders near the top of the talus slope
Are so huge and tossed they create
Caves and passages to other caves
Of cool shade and the buzz of wasp wings.
There, at the base of the trickle, we stand
In a veritable cloud of wasps, yet are not
Threatened until we begin to encroach
On the water, on their source,
At which their drone assonates
Anger, their flight quickens,
Their navigation becomes an erratic intimidation.
These insects could inject a lethal dose.
Down farther, on the heated boulders,
Rattlesnakes sun and don't give a damn
About us either as we pass by.

Two men once slept in this canyon,
And early in the moonlit night, a figure
Presided in noncommittal fashion
Over their conversation of subjects
Lost and mystical. This figure
They perceived not by staring directly,
But from the corners of their perceptions,
As if the light that reflected from the form
Appeared as that around it appeared,
With all unsightly edges carefully blurred over.
It was a blot upon the eye.
It was a chameleon ability
On the order of light manipulation.
It was an effect circumscribed
And circumvented by peripheral vision,
For where the light was dim

On sight's edge, where vision
Is stripped of all color,
The figure could be seen.
The figure was of a man,
About sixty in appearance,
Brown-skinned, grizzled, short,
Stocky, serape over a shoulder,
Sombrero thrown over the back.
The eyes were either black holes
Or points of glitter.
It was a bush
When the two looked directly at it.
Neither man spoke or otherwise gave
The other hint of its presence,
Yet both, aware, felt it near,
Saw it observe, and realized
Its absence when, as silently
As it had come, it had gone.

We trudged, at last, up the dry creek bed
As it wandered from the lower canyon,
Lost and searching for deeper channels.
The sun already was disappearing behind
The mesa, the air rapidly growing cool.
We unrolled our bedding, settled wearily
Down for food, rest, quiet talk, and perhaps....

What words can I use to describe
The way the moonlight twisted
In fragments of sharp light splitting
Like a kaleidoscope of prisms
Shattered when I tried to look

At a particular spot near me?
The full moon shone from its dark,
Spangled canopy. The mesa wall,
The brush, the rocks all around
Showed clearly in its glow. All save
A spot near a large mesquite.
That spot twisted my eyes from itself,
Rolled them up inside my head.
I could not look there....
Can I hope to explain? My eyes
Were unable to remain fixed upon
That spot, were unable because
That spot held so potent
A force of illusion my mind
Refused to focus on such a reality.
Incomprehensible in is mere referents,
It was to my sight an impossibility of vision
On the scale of Technicolor to Braille.
The colors were neither gaudy nor bright—
I believe they were within my eye alone,
As if something stuck a spoon of confusion
Through the pupil, into the bowl of my eye,
And stirred the rods and cones it found there.
Sometime later, I sank
Into a sleep of darkness
Unnatural in its depth and weight.
No one had spoken. No one was seen.

We shot more than thirty photographs
Of the canyon and its approach,
Yet none developed.
This is, to me, of small consequence—

The canyon's appearance is burned hard
Into my memory, is a black
Scar traversing now forgotten dreams
Of power and thoughts on the nature
Of reality. It is a place I fear
And know I must return to,
A place of charged energy evident
In the mad drone of thousands of wasps
And splinters of vision colored,
Shaped, and manipulated by something that
My failure to see much less understand
Leaves me indecisive and yearning.

To Abajo we returned the next day,
To our vehicle with cruise control
And the power of the greatest cities
Man has known, the mightiest technology.
Yet the air is stinking, and our greatest
Order of light manipulation lies
In movie houses.
At the first human habitation,
We asked about the canyon, were told
Its name. Later, recrossing the Pecos,
Staring at the Indian's cave devoid
Of artifacts, robbed of its bones,
I recalled the canyon's name—Bruja Canyon—
And remembered its darkness and its light.

Phosphene Publishing Company publishes books
and DVDs related to literature, drama, history,
Texana, film, the paranormal,
spirituality, and the martial arts.

For other great titles, visit

phosphenepublishing.com

4.1-12/25

www.ingramcontent.com/pod-product-compliance
Lightning Source LLC
Chambersburg PA
CBHW061448040426
42450CB00007B/1264